Tortoises

Kate Riggs

CREATIVE EDUCATION • CREATIVE PAPERBACKS

seedlings

Published by Creative Education and Creative Paperbacks
P.O. Box 227, Mankato, Minnesota 56002
Creative Education and Creative Paperbacks
are imprints of The Creative Company
www.thecreativecompany.us

Design by Ellen Huber; production by Joe Kahnke
Art direction by Rita Marshall
Printed in the United States of America

Photographs by Alamy (All Canada Photos, Martin Harvey),
Dreamstime (Bornin54, Tracy Hebden, Isselee, Mihail
Ivanov, Jdanne, Oleg Kozlov, Leisuretime70, Mary981,
Matthewgsimpson, Mattiaath, Mgkuijpers, Smileus,
Angelique Van Heertum, Vselenka, Wcpmedia), iStockphoto
(EcoPic, filo, hocus-focus, PetrP), Shutterstock (EcoPrint,
fivespots, JI de Wet), SuperStock (Gerard Lacz/age fotostock)

Library of Congress Cataloging-in-Publication Data
Riggs, Kate.
Tortoises / Kate Riggs.
p. cm. — (Seedlings)
Includes bibliographical references and index.
Summary: A kindergarten-level introduction to tortoises,
covering their growth process, behaviors, the habitats they
call home, and such defining features as their rounded shells.
ISBN 978-1-60818-740-9 (hardcover)
ISBN 978-1-62832-336-8 (pbk)
ISBN 978-1-56660-775-9 (eBook)
1. Testudinidae—Juvenile literature.
2. Turtles—Juvenile literature.
QL666.C584 R54 2016
597.92/4—dc23   2015041986
CCSS: RI.K.1, 2, 3, 4, 5, 6, 7;
RI.1.1, 2, 3, 4, 5, 6, 7; RF.K.1, 3; RF.1.1

First Edition HC 9 8 7 6 5 4 3 2 1
First Edition PBK 9 8 7 6 5 4 3 2 1

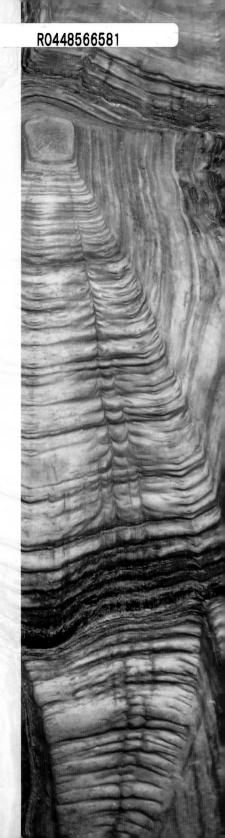

TABLE OF CONTENTS

Hello, tortoises!

Tortoises are animals
that move slowly.
They live on land.

Some tortoises are found on islands.

Tortoises have rounded shells.

The top of the shell is hard. The bottom part is softer.

Strong-legged
tortoises dig
holes.

They use their front feet and claws.

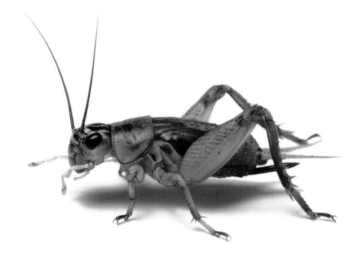

Tortoises eat leaves, grasses, and flowers. Sometimes they eat bugs and worms.

A baby tortoise comes out of an egg. It is called a hatchling.

The hatchling looks for food. It lives by itself.

Quiet tortoises live alone.

They look for food. They warm up in the sun.

Goodbye, tortoises!

shell

foot

claw

nostril

eye

beak

skin

leg

21

Words to Know

claws: curved nails on the toes of some animals

islands: pieces of land surrounded by water

Index

Read More

Dunphy, Madeleine. *At Home with the Gopher Tortoise: The Story of a Keystone Species.*
Berkeley, Calif.: Web of Life Children's Books, 2010.

Schuetz, Kari. *Reptiles.*
Minneapolis: Bellwether Media, 2013.

Websites

San Diego Turtle and Tortoise Society: Videos
http://www.sdturtle.org/#!video/c1bf2
Watch videos about desert tortoises and other kinds.

Tortoise and Turtle Preschool Activities and Crafts
http://www.first-school.ws/theme/animals/reptiles/turtle.htm
Print out activity sheets and read a story about a tortoise
that raced a hare.